REFLECTIONS
FOR
YOUNG PEOPLE

Patrick T. Reardon

ACTA

Starting Out
Reflections for Young People
Patrick T. Reardon

Edited by Gregory F. Augustine Pierce
Cover design by James Lemons
Typesetting by Garrison Publications

Scripture quotations are from the New Revised
Standard Version of the Bible, copyright © 1989
by the Division of Christian Education of the
National Council of the Churches of Christ in the
U.S.A. Used with permission. All rights reserved.

Published by: ACTA Publications
          Assisting Christians To Act
          4848 N. Clark Street
          Chicago, IL 60640-4711
          773-271-1030
          E-mail: ACTApublications@aol.com

Library of Congress Catalog Number: 00-101208
ISBN: 0-87946-212-4
Year: 05 04 03 02 01 00
Printing 8 7 6 5 4 3 2 1 First Printing
Printed in the United States of America

With love, to Cathy,
and
for David and Sarah
who are starting out in the world,
and

for Kelly

Introduction

Each dawn is new. Each morning is fresh and filled with possibilities.

Your days—today, tomorrow and the next—are spread out ahead of you. That can be a scary thought. After all, no one can tell you what life will bring your way. You will go down roads you can't even envision now. You will meet the unlikeliest of people and go through the most unexpected experiences.

The thing to remember is that your life is an adventure. And it's *your* adventure.

You will have a lot to say about what roads you go down, and what people you meet, and what experiences you have. You will have a lot to say about how vibrant your life is. And how fruitful.

Will you drink life deeply? Or will you turn your head away, for fear the taste will be a little odd? It's up to you. This is your life and your adventure.

You stand at an exciting moment.

Sure, there are risks. Sure, there will be painful times, and you will be hurt, and you will have sorrows. But there will also be unexpected delights, wonderful surprises and rich loves.

There is a wonderful life waiting to unfold for you—courtesy of God and of all the people of the world.

Be Eager

Be eager. Be excited. Enjoy.

Don't ignore what's wrong with the world and what's bad in your own life. Work for change.

But don't ignore the beauty in your life.

And the sheer wonder of it all.

My soul magnifies the Lord, and my spirit rejoices in God my Savior.—Luke 1:46-47

Far-Fetched

In the Bible, God, in the guise of a traveler, visits Abraham in the desert. And, as Sarah stands eavesdropping just inside the tent's entryway, the Lord tells Abraham that he and Sarah, both aged and barren, will have a son.

Sarah laughs.

God understands. Some things seem far-fetched.

Nine months later, Isaac is born.

I never came upon any of my discoveries through the process of rational thinking.
—Albert Einstein

Sunrise

Romance is like the dawn.

It suffuses your life with light.

It warms you. It makes all the world richer, fuller.

Unlike the sun, romance—for all its storms—never has to set.

Love and a cough cannot be hid.
—George Herbert

Finding a First Job

For one thing, it's like winning a prize when you get a job. You're good enough! They want you. They need you.

For another, you're on your way. You're beginning a career.

Sure, this first job may be a false start or a dead end. There may be several false starts.

But you're on your way. You're finding out (and deciding) who you are and who you will be.

To labor is to pray.
—St. Benedict

Life and Death

Life is filled with surprise.

You will be surprised at when—and with whom—you fall in love.

You will be amazed at the obstacles you will be able to overcome in your everyday life.

You will be astonished at how, with a word, with a gentle touch, you will be able to ease another's pain or fill another with wild joy.

Even death will be surprising. (Think of the Resurrection.)

Trust in God: She will provide.
—Emmeline Pankhurst

Dream

Peace is possible.

Work for justice.

Be open.

Love.

With this faith we will be able to work together, to pray together, to struggle together, to go to jail together, to stand up for freedom together, knowing that we will be free one day. This will be the day when all of God's children will be able to sing with new meaning—"My country 'tis of thee; sweet land of liberty, of thee I sing; land where my fathers died, land of the pilgrim's pride, from every mountain side, let freedom ring."
—Martin Luther King, Jr.

God Was There

In the Bible, Elijah goes to the mountain to meet God.

And there was a great wind. But God was not in the wind.

And there was a great earthquake. But God was not in the earthquake.

And there was a great fire. But God was not in the fire.

Then, there was a gentle breeze. A whisper, really.

And God was there with Elijah.

Go out and stand on the mountain before the Lord, for the Lord is about to pass by.
—1 Kings 19:11

Commercials

Don't get fooled into thinking that the commercials on TV or the ads on billboards or in magazines reflect any sort of reality.

The best way to think of these things is as fantasies of a make-believe world. It's a world that's enough like ours that it seems familiar, but it's also weirdly perfect. There is no problem that cannot be solved, no pain that cannot be alleviated, no whim that cannot be fulfilled. The fantasy is so well-conceived and well-produced that it's easy to be tricked.

Don't try to live in this fantasy land. The only way you can do so is by turning your life into a fantasy.

Oh, had our simple Eve seen through the make-believe! Had she but known the Pretender he was!—Ralph Hodgson

The Tortoise
and the Hare

The tortoise and the hare had a race.

The hare ran very fast. The tortoise ran slow and steady.

The hare won. No one was surprised.

The surprise was that the tortoise agreed to race in the first place.

"Why not?" the tortoise said. "What did I have to lose?"

Our doubts are traitors, and make us lose the good we oft might win, by fearing to attempt.—William Shakespeare

Passion

Art is passion. Faith is passion. Sex is passion. Love is passion. Joy is passion. Work is passion.

Passion is the electricity that sparks everything human.

Passion is God's Spirit. Passion is holy.

Prayer is passion.

The word of the Lord falls with the force of a snowflake.—William Sloane Coffin

Shadrach, Meshach and Abednego

In the Bible, the three true believers refuse to worship a golden idol and are thrown into a fiery furnace by the evil king. God saves them.

The flames are so intense that the king's henchmen are burned up, but Shadrach, Meshach and Abednego don't even break a sweat. Instead, God sends a breeze to cool them, and they sing a song of praise to the Lord. They have a party in the furnace, the wildest, most unexpected of parties. And the king watches in awe—at the work of a King much greater than he ever imagined.

But the children of Israel would not bow down. Shadrach, Meshach, Abednego. / Couldn't fool 'em with the golden idol. Shadrach, Meshach, Abednego.
—Robert MacGimsey

Express Yourself

Express yourself. Risk showing who you really are.

Our culture trains us to be deceitful. To pretend we're like everyone else. To hide our idiosyncrasies and our feelings and our ideas and our character from sight. We're told in TV commercial after TV commercial, in billboard after billboard, that there are cool ways to be. And all other ways are wrong.

But trust yourself. Be strong in your sense of your self. Your individuality. Know that who you are and what you have to say are important and worthwhile.

> *Dare to be naive.*
> —R. Buckminster Fuller

Alone

There's nothing like growing up for learning what it feels like to be alone.

You're on your own when you start your first job, when you get your first apartment (even with roommates), when you move to a new city, when you sit down for the first time to a meal for one.

These experiences can be deeply lonely. But they can also be quietly pleasurable.

Being alone is good and bad—often at the same time.

We live as we dream—alone.
—Joseph Conrad

The Twelve Rabbits—1

The twelve rabbits were rehearsing a play. And everything was going wrong—scenery was falling, actors were forgetting their lines, no one was paying attention.

"It's all Sally Rabbit's fault," one of the rabbits said. "That's right," said another. So the other eleven rabbits made fun of Sally and blamed her and snubbed her and made her cry.

And scenery kept falling. Actors kept forgetting their lines. And there was still no one paying attention.

I beg you to lead a life worthy of the calling to which you have been called, with all humility and gentleness, with patience, bearing with one another in love, making every effort to maintain the unity of the Spirit in the bond of peace.—Ephesians 4:1-3

The Twelve Rabbits—2

The twelve rabbits were rehearsing a play. And everything was going wrong—scenery was falling, actors were forgetting their lines, no one was paying attention. "It's all Sally Rabbit's fault," one of the rabbits said.

"No," said another. "We're all to blame. Let's work together, and we can get things straightened out."

"OK," said the others, and they figured out how to keep the scenery in place, and they remembered their lines, and everyone paid attention when the director spoke.

> *There is one body and one Spirit.*
> *—Ephesians 4:4*

Tomorrow

Don't be in a hurry to grow up.

Be silly. Take time to waste time with people you like. Laugh. Dance. Sing, even if you're off-key.

Let tomorrow take care of tomorrow.

We should consider every day lost on which we have not danced at least once.
—Friedrich Nietzsche

The Trials of Job

In the Bible, God afflicts Job with boils. God takes away Job's riches and kills off Job's family.

Job is angry and bitter.

"Why?" he demands.

God says: "I am God! What do you know?"

God is subtle, but not malicious.
—Albert Einstein

Strive

Ambition is the fuel of progress. But it can also bend and twist your life completely out of shape.

Some things are worth striving for. It's important to stretch, to reach. It's important to be the best you can be. But be careful you aren't warped by the effort.

You have to keep your ambition in perspective. You have to stay in balance.

Striving to better, oft we mar what's well.
—*William Shakespeare*

Don't Settle

Some jobs are mind-numbingly boring. Or stressful. Or draining.

But you don't have to settle for that kind of job.

Do what you can to find a job that at least is interesting for you. Or, even better, fun.

Find a job you can do well. Find one that's meaningful.

We're talking about a third of your life here.

The soul should always stand ajar, ready to
welcome the ecstatic experience.
—*Emily Dickinson*

Filled with Wonder

Some people are young when they have children. Others are middle-aged.

Being a parent is not a second job. It's your most important job for the twenty years or so that it takes to raise a child.

Parenting is the most stressful, irritating, exhausting, soul-shaking, scary, mind-rattling, challenging, mystifying, humbling experience you'll ever face.

It is also filled with wonder.

A baby's smile. A son's hug. A daughter's driving lay-up during a school basketball game. The rewards far outweigh the costs.

Who could ask for anything more?
—George and Ira Gershwin

Take a Walk

Take walks. Stretch your legs. Leave the car at home. You see more of life that way.

And don't put headphones over your ears.

Listen to the sound of leaves rustling in the wind. And birds. And children. And traffic. And airplanes overhead.

And someone walking past you, saying, "Hi!"

Ninety percent of life is just showing up.
—Woody Allen

Heroes

Heroes are good to have. They show you that greatness is possible.

But success is only one side of the coin.

Don't be disappointed when you discover that your hero isn't perfect.

A hero is a human being. And human beings fail. We have our blind spots. We make errors. We hurt each other.

Your hero isn't perfect. And neither will you be when, at some future time—and, don't worry, it will come—you are a hero to some young person starting out.

It has been my experience that folks who have no vices have very few virtues.
—Abraham Lincoln

Be Kind

Be kind. That may seem like overly sweet advice, but, once you're out in the world, you'll see how pervasive unkindness can be.

You'll meet people who are rude and who back-bite and slander and denigrate and sneer and play favorites and enjoy inflicting pain.

Not everyone's this way, not by a long shot. But, if you're not careful, you can be sucked into this unkind approach to life.

Instead, be kind to everyone. Be gracious. Be courteous, gentle, attentive.

Don't be afraid to be nice. It's a happy sort of rebellion against the way of the world.

A gentle tongue is a tree of life.
—Proverbs 15:4

Articulate

If you watch much TV, you can feel that you don't measure up.

On TV shows, everyone's articulate. We feel tongue-tied next to them. Stupid, even.

In real life, the dialogue isn't crafted by a scriptwriter. We write our own lines.

But don't worry if the words seem awkward. Don't be concerned if you grope for ways to explain how you feel or what you think.

The important thing is to let people know who you are.

Don't compromise yourself. You are all you've got.—Janis Joplin

Happy

There was a serious young man who climbed a high mountain to consult a wise man who lived near the peak.

The wise man didn't look so wise. He was dressed in everyday clothes. He was doing chores around his small wood house when the young man arrived. And he was so jovial that his visitor grew annoyed.

"How can you be so happy when the world is so filled with pain?" the visitor asked.

"Because the sun rises," the wise one responded. "I breathe. And you, young man, have come to visit me."

A light heart lives long.
—William Shakespeare

Control

Being neat is fine. Even commendable.

Being messy also has its charm.

All lives are a mix of both.

Those parts of our lives that are neat give us a sense of being in control.

Those that are messy are reminders that much of our lives is beyond our control.

At birth we come, at death we go, bearing nothing.—Chinese proverb

Land of Milk and Honey

It won't be a place—or a state of mind—without pain, without struggle, without discomfort.

But, when you reach the land of milk and honey, you'll know you're there.

It'll be where you are loved and where you love. It'll be where your work has substance and meaning—a place rich with delight and laughter and challenge.

You will find harmony there with others. With Nature. And with God.

You will be yourself.

I've seen the promised land...And I'm happy tonight. I'm not worried about anything.
—Martin Luther King Jr.

Rocking God to Sleep

Picture God as a mother.

She gives birth to us. She nurses us. She feeds us, dries our tears, hugs us, consoles us, rocks us to sleep, sings us lullabies.

Picture God as a father. As a brother. As a sister. As a daughter. As a son.

Picture God as a baby. Can you picture rocking God to sleep?

I believe in the incomprehensibility of God.
—*Honore Balzac*

Life on the Edge

In the Bible, Jesus avoided the power-brokers. He hung around, instead, with little people—fishermen, spinsters, tax collectors, prostitutes.

These were people out of step with the culture of the time—people on the outside looking in.

Jesus lived—and died—on the edges of society.

There's a message there.

If Jesus Christ were to come today, people would not even crucify him. They would ask him to dinner, and hear what he had to say, and make fun of it.—Thomas Carlyle

A Secret

Here's a secret: Humor is a big part of love. Not cut-downs, or sarcasm, or ridicule. But a shared laughter.

Lovers laugh so much because they're giddy. Love is always a surprise. It seems to come from nowhere. It's not earned. It's free. It's a surrender. In a world that honors power and force, love is the silliest thing imaginable.

Lovers know this. They laugh at their good fortune.

Something there is about you that strikes a match in me.—Bob Dylan

Losing

Losing is never easy—at least it shouldn't be.

If you don't care about winning, why play the game?

But, if you care too much, the game is warped. It's not a game any more.

You have to play the game, knowing you might lose. You have to try to win, knowing you might fail.

Losing is a bitter pill. But it's part of life.

Without losing, winning wouldn't be as sweet.

Success and failure are both greatly overrated. But failure gives you a whole lot more to talk about.—Hildegard Knef

Thank You

Be a spendthrift when it comes to thanks.

Be extravagant with your gratitude.

Giving thanks closes a circle. It helps you remember that what you've accomplished wasn't done alone. And it gives those who helped you a share in your success.

Think of thanks as a seasoning at the meal of life. It makes everything taste better.

Gratitude is heaven itself.
—William Blake

Violence

Jane slaps Sally in the face. That's violent.

Jane tricks Sally into buying much more life insurance than she needs. That's violent.

Jane fires Sally and ten thousand other workers in her company to boost earnings and improve the value of her stock options. That's violent.

Violence does not and cannot exist by itself;
it is invariably intertwined with the lie.
—Alexander Solzhenitsyn

Community

Public transportation can be a pain, whether it's the bus or subway. Taking any public conveyance, even a plane or a train, can be an irritation. You can't just pick up and go as you can with a car. There's also, of course, the crowding. Even when a bus or plane cabin isn't over-crowded, you're not alone. You're with other people. You see them; they see you.

This isn't completely bad. It's a reminder—one that's impossible to miss—that you're a member of the human community in all its often wonderful, but sometimes frustrating, diversity.

Do not try to persuade yourselves that you can do anything good on your own; on the contrary, do all in common; one prayer, one petition, one mind, one hope in the unity of love and in innocent joy—this is Jesus Christ than whom there is nothing higher.
—St. Ignatius of Antioch

Team Work

Teamwork is not just a strategy for achieving success on the job. It's also a mirror of life.

An office staff, a work crew, even an entire company — all of these are communities.

A community thrives if its members work together to reach a goal. Even more, it blossoms if its members care for each other.

Microsoft is a community—for better or worse. So is the local McDonald's.

And, as an employee, you help make your work community life-giving...or dysfunctional.

God has no hands but our hands and no
tongue but our tongue.
—Annie Johnson Flint

Love

Love is not play, although play is a part of love. Love is not something that falls on you, or that you fall into. At least, not long-lasting love. There's an element of work to love. You have to work at being with someone. You have to work to be your real self. And you have to work to see, to really see, your partner.

Love is reaching out, always reaching out. You're reaching out to reveal the fullness of yourself to your partner. And you're reaching out to see and understand and know the fullness of your partner.

Love is not a game. It is the sun and the moon and the stars.

We can only learn to love by loving.
—*Iris Murdoch*

Finding God

So, you're running down the court on a fast break. You're flying! Your body is operating without conscious thought.

You cut, take the pass, fake, leap, double-pump and scoop the ball under the defender's flailing arms, up against the backboard, and into the basket.

In the clarity of the moment, in the pure unspoken communication of you and your teammates, in the union of discipline and abandon, in a body trained and then set free to fly—there, right there, is a glimmer of God.

If anything is sacred, the human body is sacred.—Walt Whitman

Learning His Trade

In the Bible, Jesus seems to have known who he was and what he was about from the very beginning. At least, that's how the gospel writers portray him. But that seems unlikely.

Don't you think Jesus had to struggle to figure out what he was called to do, just like any young person?

Don't you think he, like any teen or young adult, pictured himself in different careers and different situations? As a carpenter? As a husband? As a father? As a rabbi?

Don't you think he had to learn to be the Messiah?

The child grew and became strong, filled with wisdom; and the favor of God was upon him.—Luke 2:40

Grass

Take time to look at grass.

Get down on the lawn and look at the blades of grass. Examine a single blade. Notice its particular shade of green. Notice how straight it is, and how flexible.

Smell newly mown grass. It's as if the soul of the earth has opened itself up to draw you in.

Lie down on your back on the grass. Let the sun warm your face. Feel the soft carpet of grass under your body.

As a child, you played in the grass. Don't ever think you have to abandon this as an adult.

The heart of a little child...pure as the Buddha.—Chinese proverb

Wind and Sun

The wind and the sun are arguing over which is the strongest.

"I'm more powerful, and I can prove it," brags the wind. "See that young man walking down that sidewalk there. Watch me blow his coat right off him!" So the wind blows and blows and blows, and nearly blows the coat away. But the young man just hugs the coat ever closer to his body.

"My turn," says the sun, covering the land with the tender warmth of its bright light. On the sidewalk, the young man stops and lifts his face to catch as many of the sun's warm rays as he can.

And then he takes off his coat.

He deserves Paradise who makes his companions laugh.—*the Koran*

In the Cemetery

Some people are superstitious about cemeteries. They avert their eyes when going past. They don't want to think about death and dying.

If life was forever, no moment would have much value.

But, since it does end—for each of us, for all of us—each moment is of immeasurable richness.

It's good to be reminded of that.

Every moment dies a man, / Every moment one is born.—Alfred Lord Tennyson

Seed

In the Bible, Jesus told of the mustard seed. Something so small, yet it holds the potential of a great tree.

No action is tiny in its potential consequences.

A kind word ripples on forever through humanity.

A harsh word, too.

> *Love is a verb.*
> —*Clare Boothe Luce*

Have Faith

Believe in something.

Be excited by life.

Avoid cynicism.

Be on fire with enthusiasm. For God. For justice. For art. For your family. For the love of your life. For yourself.

Believe in yourself.

That is happiness: to be dissolved into something complete and great.
—Willa Cather

Tree-Climber

In the Bible, Zacchaeus lived a bad life, cheating people as a tax collector. Then, one day, he heard that Jesus was coming to town. But when Zacchaeus went out to the road to see him, the crowd was too thick, and Zacchaeus was too short. He didn't give up. Instead, he climbed a tree to see Jesus—and, in the process, found salvation. Jesus came to his house and showed him how to live better.

Zacchaeus knew he needed something. And, once he had a glimmer of where he could find it, he didn't waste time going after it. The moral is simple: When you see your chance, grab it.

It usually happens that the more faithfully a person follows the inspirations he receives, the more does he experience new inspirations which ask increasingly more of him.
—Joseph de Guibert

Failed

It is human to fail—to drop the ball, to blow the sale, to get the facts wrong, to mix the ingredients incorrectly, to say the wrong word, to break the vase, to spill the oil, to scratch the paint, to run out of gas, to arrive late, to sing off-key, to cut the fabric raggedly, to miscalculate, to stumble, to overlook, to miss, to fall, to err.

OK, so you've failed.

Welcome to the human race.

You may be disappointed if you fail, but you are doomed if you don't try.—Beverly Sills

Bad Boss

The sparrow said to the squirrel: "My boss is bad. She nit-picks and criticizes and ridicules. I hate my job."

The squirrel said: "Look for a new job."

"I can't," said the sparrow. "I'm afraid I'll get a worse job. Besides, I need the money."

"How much," the squirrel asked, "is your happiness worth?"

Without work, all life goes rotten, but when work is soulless, life stifles and dies.
—Albert Camus

A Formula

Attend. Pay heed. Listen. Note. Keep your eyes open. Hear. Watch. Look. Study. Examine. Feel. Ponder. Consider. Contemplate. Analyze. Savor. Weigh.

Then talk.

Don't ever talk until you know what you're talking about.—Sam Rayburn

Prayer

In the Bible, Jesus prays in the Garden of Olives.

He also prays over the water at the marriage feast in Cana.

And he prays over the Torah in his hometown synagogue.

Even more, his life is a prayer. Each breath he draws is a prayer. Each word he says, each step he takes, is a prayer.

It is a prayer because he is alert to and aware of the fullness of life and the source of that life—his (and our) Father.

Let my prayer be counted as incense before you, and the lifting up of my hands as an evening sacrifice.—Psalm 141: 2

Perfect

Life isn't perfect. And nothing in life is perfect. Even when you score a great triumph—make a big sale, win an important game, finish a major project. Even when you fall in love with someone for whom you care deeply and who cares deeply about you.

When you think you should be totally content, there will be a restlessness. When you think you should be totally happy, there will be a touch of sadness.

Don't worry. This is the way life is.

The flipside, of course, is that, even in dark times, when your sorrow and pain are their greatest, there is still the sunrise.

Life is a succession of moments. To live each one is to succeed.—Corita Kent

Two Sisters

In the Bible, Martha cooks the meals, sweeps the floors and does the rest of the housework while Mary, her sister, sits and listens to Jesus teach.

Is one way better than the other?

It would be a sterile life to have housework without the beauty, challenge and wonder of faith.

But what sort of life would it be if no one cooked?

> *Pray to God, but row for the shore.*
> *—Russian proverb*

Nurturing

Nourish something. Plant a garden. Raise a child. Keep a pet. Have dreams.

Slow down enough to witness the almost imperceptible changes that make up life: A green shoot, reaching for the sky, suddenly blossoms. A child, learning her words, speaks her first sentence.

Take in the beauty of a dog running across the grass, legs in rhythm, body and being centered on the moment and the movement.

Nourish that beauty. Raise a puppy. Teach a young girl her words. Get your hands down in the soil—planting, weeding and nurturing.

The Lord will guide you continually...and you shall be like a watered garden, like a spring of water, whose waters never fail.
—*Isaiah 58:11*

Doubt

Doubt deeply, and believe strongly.

Challenge common assumptions. Pose difficult questions. Examine motives—your own and those of others.

But, also, commit yourself. Take a stand. Find meaning in life.

Be a skeptical believer. A believing skeptic.

Great doubts, deep wisdom...small doubts, little wisdom.—Chinese proverb

The Lioness
and the Mouse~1

The lioness grabs the mouse and is going to eat it. But the mouse shouts, "Wait! Let me go! I don't taste good. Besides, someday, I may be able to help you."

The idea seems so silly that the lioness laughs and laughs and loses her grip on the mouse, and the mouse scurries away.

The moral: Speak up for yourself.

Not knowing when the dawn will come, I open every door.—Emily Dickinson

The Lioness
and the Mouse~2

Later, the lioness steps on a bramble and gets a thorn lodged in her paw. The lioness roars in anger and pain, and none of the animals in the forest will come near her.

Except the mouse.

"Go away!" the lioness shouts, embarrassed at her weakness. But the mouse comes closer and, using his teeth, gently extracts the thorn from the lioness's paw.

The moral: Someone weak today may be strong tomorrow. (Or, more simply, be nice to everyone.)

Happiness is something that comes into our lives through doors we don't even remember leaving open.—Rose Lane

Sex and Love

Sex is something powerful.

It is, of course, an evolutionary drive, hard-wired into each of us, for the perpetuation of the human species. It is a pleasure.

But it is richest when it is an act of love. Then, it is a dance. It is a conversation. It is a celebration.

And something more. It is not just an expression of love but a fostering of love as well. It not only shows that love is present, but also feeds that love—makes it stronger, deeper, richer.

Love breeds love.

I am my beloved's and my beloved is mine.—Song of Solomon 6:3

Gift

Sometimes, giving a gift can be as good, or better, than getting one.

If I really know you, and really know who you are and what you like, I can pick out a gift that is just right. It will surprise and please you. Even more, you will be surprised and pleased at how well I know you.

You will not only enjoy the gift, you will enjoy the realization that I have cared enough about you to really know you.

And here's the thing: I will enjoy your enjoyment. Your enjoyment will be a gift from you to me.

A man there was, though some did count him mad, the more he cast away the more he had.—John Bunyan

Emotions

Notice how you feel. Be aware of your emotions. Don't hold in. Don't hold back. Express yourself.

Laugh. Sing. Cry. Shout. Dance. Coo. Giggle. Whisper.

Hug. Kiss.

Be yourself. Be alive.

Don't hide. Show yourself.

> *Love the moment, and the energy of that moment will spread beyond all boundaries.—Corita Kent*

The Road Taken

George Rabbit left his family's home one day to make his way in the world. A short distance down the road, he came to a place where the road split off in two directions. One went east; the other, west. He took one of the forks.

A short way down the road, he came to another place where the road split off in two directions. He took one of the forks.

And so it went.

Just before he died, he was standing at the end of a road, trying to decide which of two forks to take.

The highest moral ideal either for a people or for an individual is to be true to its destiny— to leave the known for the unknown.
—Christopher Dawson

Second-Guess Yourself

Question yourself. Second-guess yourself. See where you've failed.

This is a skill.

You have to be careful, though, not to over-do it. If you second-guess yourself too much, you won't make any moves for fear of failure.

Recognize that failure is part of life. And recognize that even when you're most loving and most successful, there are ways you fall short.

The key is to avoid complacency. And self-satisfaction.

> *Life is change. Growth is optional.*
> *Choose wisely.—Karen Kaiser Clark*

A Choice

Find a job with meaning. The more meaning it has, the more it will seem worth your while to do it.

What is meaning?

Are people better because of the service or product you provide? Does it feed them? Or clothe them? Or give them happiness? Or fill their lives with beauty?

Most jobs have meaning. Some, more than others.

You have a choice.

The only happy people I know are the ones who are working well at something they consider important.—Abraham Maslow

The Whale

In the Bible, Jonah lived in the whale three days.

In there, he contemplated God's call.

He hadn't wanted to do what he'd been called to do—to preach to the people of a wicked city.

The whale was God's way of getting Jonah's attention.

> *Doubt is part of all religion. All the religious thinkers were doubters.*
> —*Isaac Bashevis Singer*

Community

Life is a fabric.

And we are all threads in that fabric.

Are you red? Or gold? Or green? The color of the sky? Of coal? Of a carrot?

We are all connected, and none of us sees the fullness of the fabric we form.

But it is bright and beautiful and wildly vibrant.

If all pulled in one direction, the world would keel over.—Yiddish proverb

The Adventure Called Life

Sarah Rabbit got up one day and said to her parents, "It's time for me to go out and find my way in the world."

The parents had known this day would come.

They were sad that they wouldn't see Sarah each morning and each evening, that she wouldn't be there to laugh with them over silly jokes, that they would no longer have a front-row seat to her life.

But they were happy because this was what Sarah had been born to do.

She was heading off on the adventure called life.

If the creator had a purpose in equipping us with a neck, he surely meant for us to stick it out.—Arthur Koestler

The Alternative

It's a chore, of course.

Something that's simple and mindless.

There's no challenge to it—no thrill of success at completing the task. Nothing to crow about.

And, once the garbage is taken out, there will be more garbage soon enough.

You do it because—well—if you don't, you end up with one of those houses that are floor-to-ceiling filled with trash.

The sum of wisdom is that the time is never lost that is devoted to work.
—Ralph Waldo Emerson

Justice and Injustice

If one person is the victim of discrimination, we all are.

If one person is ridiculed, we all are.

If one person is shunned, we all are.

A world unjust to anyone is a world unjust to you and me.

And when this happens, when we allow freedom to ring, when we let it ring from every village and every hamlet, from every state and every city, we will be able to speed up that day when all of God's children—black men and white men, Jews and Gentiles, Protestants and Catholics—will be able to join hands and sing in the words of the old Negro spiritual, "Free at last! Free at last! Thank God Almighty, we are free at last!"—Martin Luther King, Jr.

Home

Home is a sanctuary in a rushing world. It's a haven of love and acceptance and comfort.

It can also be a prison.

Don't hide at home out of fear of life. God is to be found at home—but also in the hurly-burly of the world.

I fled Him, down the nights and down the days; / I fled Him, down the arches of the years; / I fled Him, down the labyrinthine ways / of my own mind; and in the midst of tears / I hid from Him, and under running laughter.—Francis Thompson

Feed the Soul

Meals are meeting places.

Meals are where people share their lives and themselves.

This is the opposite of eating on the run. It's the antithesis of a TV dinner.

A meal is sacred in this way. It's where people come together, where love happens.

As you feed the body, you feed the soul.

They told what had happened on the road, and how Jesus had been made known to them in the breaking of the bread.
—Luke 24:35

Tree

Plant a tree.

As a gift to someone. Or to everyone.

Watch the tree grow. Watch it move through the seasons—grow green in spring, turn brown in autumn, stand bare amid the snow of winter.

And then grow green again.

A tree reaches to the sky and is rooted to the earth.

Not a bad symbol for living a full life.

Nature does have manure and she does have roots as well as blossoms, and you can't hate the manure and blame the roots for not being blossoms.—R. Buckminster Fuller

Poison

In the Bible, Salome dances to please Herod.

He offers her anything she wants.

At the urging of her mother—the King's courtesan, long criticized by John the Baptist—she asks for John's head on a platter.

And so she gets it.

Then what does she do with it? She gives it to her mother. The perfect gift.

Their grapes are grapes of poison, their clusters are bitter; their wine is the poison of serpents, the cruel venom of asps.
—Deuteronomy 32: 32-33

Evangelize

You preach the gospel—you tell the world what you believe—by how you live.

If you are cold to people, you preach of a cold God. If your heart is hard, you preach of a hard-hearted God.

But, if you are kind, respectful, thoughtful, helpful, attentive, modest, solid, gentle— well, that's a sort of Eden you preach, isn't it?

To be able to practice five things everywhere under heaven constitutes perfect virtue— gravity, generosity of soul, sincerity, earnestness and kindness.—Confucius

Emptiness

There is good emptiness and bad emptiness.

It is good at times in your life to feel empty—to feel drained or used up or without inspiration or joy. This is part of the cycle of life. The great ones compare this to being in a desert. In these desert times, you struggle with the meaning of life and the meaning of your life. You will get through these dry periods and reach fruitful times.

The bad emptiness is when you're too afraid of getting hurt to really live. If you don't risk new people and new experiences and new ideas, you are hiding out. And, in the end, you will have lived an empty life.

Do you have the stuff to seek what you love
and cultivate it and pass it on?
—Michael Ventura

Help

Ask for help.

If you're moving, ask for help. If you're lost, ask directions. If you can't figure out your income tax forms or your car engine or a cookbook recipe, admit it.

When you ask someone for help, it's a compliment.

It's also a reminder that we're all in this together.

Our help is in the name of the Lord, who made heaven and earth.—Psalm 124:8

Largesse

Volunteer at a soup kitchen, sure. Stand on street corners to help raise money for those who are needy, of course.

But, even more, don't be a prisoner of your class. Don't lock yourself within your income bracket.

Talk to everyone—poor and rich, educated and uneducated, glib and tongue-tied, conservative and liberal. Realize that every person has a story, has some new way for you to see life. And each person you meet will have a richer life by hearing your story and understanding your way of seeing life.

Be open to everyone and to everyone's largesse.

He flattered himself on being a man without any prejudices; and this pretension itself is a very great prejudice.—Anatole France

Deception at Work

When it comes to work, don't trick people.

Be straight-forward. Be direct.

You can succeed without deceit. You *really* can—even if colleagues tell you it's impossible.

And if you can't do well without the tricks, find yourself another job.

> *There are no tricks in plain and simple faith.*—William Shakespeare

Deception in Love

When it comes to love, avoid deceit.

Be straight-forward. Be direct.

A relationship built on trickery is doomed.

Love can't live on lies.

True love—the kind we ordinarily attribute
to God—is foolish, risky and absolutely
necessary. It brings to a standstill the
ordinary games of mistrust.
—Gail McGrew Eifnig

Comfortable
with Discomfort

Read difficult books. Make friends with someone complex and unpredictable. Go one-on-one against a better player.

Be comfortable with discomfort.

Not for the sake of discomfort—not at all.

But be willing to learn more, to understand more, to experience more—to add to the richness of your life—by trying new things.

Don't do hard things because they're hard. But don't let difficulties keep you from being alive.

Historically, risk-takers are people who shatter the illusion of knowledge. They are willing to try something that everyone thinks is outrageous or stupid.—Daniel J. Boorstein

Where God Is

In the Bible, Moses saw God in a burning bush.

That's an odd place to find God.

Like finding God in a Wendy's hamburger. Or a lug wrench. Or a glass of Budweiser. Or a toll booth. Or a comic book. Or your Uncle Fred.

Odd places, to be sure. But, if you look close enough at life—at any aspect of life—you'll find God.

In a lug wrench, even in your Uncle Fred—God is there.

God has nothing to give you that he is not giving you right now.—Joel Goldsmith

Understand Others

When you make fun of someone, you seem smart.

But it's such a thin, sour way to live. And it sets you apart from every person and every thing you ridicule.

A fuller, albeit more difficult, way to live is to try to understand others.

If someone fails, it's not just a failure. Often, it's a measure of how much was attempted—a credit, in a way, to the courage to try.

And, always, it's a reminder of our own tendency to fail. In many ways, we should feel closer to losers than to winners. We know their sorrow.

Forebear to judge, for we are sinners all!
—William Shakespeare

See It All

The glass isn't half-full. And it isn't half-empty.

The glass is half-full *and* half-empty.

Life is never so dark that there is no light. And it's never so joyous that there is no pain.

The secret is to see it all.

Man always travels along precipices. His truest obligation is to keep his balance.
—*Pope John Paul II*

Compromise

Don't compromise.

Have strong beliefs, strong ideas, strong feelings. Stand up for what you believe. Live life as *you* think it ought to be lived.

Of course, compromise is an important part of life. You can't—and shouldn't—always have your way when it comes to deciding what movie to go to or what color car to buy.

But, on the big stuff, don't give in. Have ethics. Have morals. Be true to yourself.

If you really believe in something, you have no choice but to go further.
—Graham Greene

The Whole World

William Rabbit lived in the field where he'd grown up. Many of his friends had left to go off and explore the world. Some came back. Others didn't.

William and his wife had many little baby rabbits who grew up and had families of their own. Some stayed in the field. Others went away.

William Rabbit died in the field where he'd grown up. "I found the whole world in this field," he said, shortly before he did.

And so he had.

What a glorious world Almighty God has given us!—Robert E. Lee

The Blessing of Flu

It may not seem this way when you're throwing up or shivering with chills or sweating from a fever. But the flu is a blessing.

It's a reminder of what an amazing and amazingly complex mechanism your body is.

And, when you get better, try to keep a memory of how bad you felt.

It will help you realize how good you now feel.

Now I am beginning to live a little, and feel less like a sick oyster at low tide.
—Louisa May Alcott

What Then?

In the Bible, Peter denied knowing Jesus once, twice, three times.

Was he wrong? Yes. Was he human? Yes.

What did he do? He spent the rest of his life affirming the message of Jesus—a message of love.

And of forgiveness.

It's human to make a mistake. The question is: What do you do then?

The more we know, the better we forgive.
Whoever feels deeply, feels for all that live.
—Madame de Stael

Field

Think of life as a field. You spend your life planting and reaping, and planting again.

You grow what you choose in the soil you have.

Your field can be beautiful and fruitful. It can be filled with brambles and fallow.

It's your field.

On Judgment Day, God will not ask to what sect you belonged, but what manner of life you led.—I.M. Kagan

Enemies or Friends

Johnny Rabbit went to his older sister. He was having a difficult time at his new job. The air seemed poisoned. People were mean to each other. Smiles were rare. Rudeness was rampant.

"Johnny," his sister said, "you can go through life looking at everyone else as your enemy. It sounds like that's the approach your coworkers are taking. Or you can go through life looking at everyone else as your friend. That's the way you should go—it's the way to a happy and full life."

And she told him one thing more: "You should probably start looking for another job."

We are not isolated souls, singular, lonely, called and engaged in a solitary effort. We are members of a great Company, and whether we think it or not, we pray in Company.—John W. Lynch

Average

The odds are, you're average.

And, even if you're talented in one particular way, you're probably pretty run-of-the-mill in others.

This is not a bad thing (despite what our culture teaches us).

No one can be excellent at everything—or, for that matter, a klutz at everything.

We're more alike than we think.

> *Betters have their betters.*
> *—Japanese proverb*

Savor Life

Savor life.

Roll it around on your tongue and taste it.

Take the time to take life in.

Listen to the Exhortation of the Dawn!
Look to this Day! For it is Life, the very
Life of Life.—Kalidasa

Nervous

The myth-makers don't tell you this, but even heroes get nervous.

Bill Russell, one of the greatest basketball players ever, used to get so anxious before a game that he would throw up right before taking the court.

Politicians, for all their experience in public life, get dry-mouthed before giving a speech. Veteran actors get scared just before the curtain goes up.

Feeling anxious, especially before doing something new or something public, is normal. It's the way we humans get ourselves ready to face a challenge.

Don't be scared about being scared.

All adventures, especially into new territory, are scary.—Sally Ride

Show-Off for God

In the Bible, Joseph has a coat of many colors.

He's a show-off for God.

It's as if he is wearing all of creation on his back—the wild diversity of life.

The moral: Celebrate life. Life is given to us to enjoy. We are made to be happy. We are made to thrill at the vibrant colors of the world, at a loved one's touch, at a simple tune. We are made for rejoicing.

Rejoice in the Lord always; again I will say, Rejoice.—Philippians 4:4

Participate

Vote. Run for office. Volunteer. Read the papers. Study the issues. Know your community. Work for justice. Demand equality. Greet your neighbors. Go to church. Use the library. Smile. Ask. Tell. Think. Act.

The spirit of history just tracked us down and used us.—John Lewis

Us-and-Them

Avoid us-and-them thinking.

There is no "them." We're all "us."

Don't think of differences—in beliefs, skin color, language, culture, income, sexual orientation, dress, education—as things that separate us.

These differences are like spices. They give life its tang.

You must learn day to day, year by year, to broaden your horizon. The more things you love, the more you are interested in, the more you enjoy, the more you are indignant about, the more you have left when anything happens.—Ethel Barrymore

The Best Policy

Be honest. Tell the truth.

It's a lot simpler that way.

You know who you are, and what you've said.

And so does everyone else.

Political language...is designed to make lies sound truthful and murder respectable, and to give the appearance of solidity to pure wind.—George Orwell

Sweet Dreams

David Rabbit leapt with joy when, early one morning, he looked outside and saw snow.

"Yeah!"

He looked forward to the fun of making snowballs. He anticipated the delight of lying down on his back and moving his arms and legs to create a snow angel.

He drank in the beauty of a world turned white.

But, then, he went back to his warm bed for some more sweet dreams.

That, too, he knew, was part of God's creation.

When one tugs at a single thing in nature,
he finds it attached to the rest of the world.
—John Muir

Who You Are

The fact is, there's a lot of your life that is out of your control.

The thing most in your control is how you treat other people.

That really is the way you determine who you are.

We will be known forever by the tracks we leave.—Native American proverb

Weather

It rains. It snows. The sun bakes down. The wind blows this way and that.

The weather is a lesson.

Life happens.

You can't argue with it. You can't control it.

Roll with the punches.

Life is what happens while we're making other plans.—John Lennon

Trust

Trust is better than suspicion.

Of course, you can't go through life without being suspicious at times. You have to protect yourself. But keep those instances to a minimum.

You don't want to be so worried about protecting yourself that you wall yourself away from everyone else.

Trust other people. Expect good from them. They will, most of them, take this as a compliment and won't disappoint you.

In fact, usually they'll surprise you with how trustworthy they are.

Treat people as if they were what they should be, and you help them become what they are capable of becoming.
—Johann Wolfgang von Goethe

The Non-Sermon on the Mount

In the Bible, at the Sermon on the Mount, Jesus did *not* say:

Blessed are the accumulators.

Blessed are those whose stocks are rising.

Blessed are the drivers of large vehicles, and the talkers on cellular phones.

Blessed are the large of ego, the cruel, the cold-blooded, the sharp-edged, the conscienceless.

Ill fares the land, to hastening ills a prey, / Where wealth accumulates, and men decay.—Oliver Goldsmith

The Sermon
on the Mount

In the Bible, at the Sermon on the Mount, Jesus *did* say:

Blessed are those who love one another.

Love is all we have, the only way that each can help the other.—Euripides

Deserts

In the Bible, Moses went into the desert.

So did John the Baptist.

And Jesus.

We all take trips to the desert from time to time. And face the barren wastes, and the hunger, and the thirst.

It's no fun.

But it's the only way to the land of milk and honey.

> *There are no shortcuts to any place worth going.—Beverly Sills*

Dignity

Do your job with dignity. Have respect for what you do, and for how it makes the world a better place.

The value of a job doesn't come from the amount of pay, or the status it brings.

The value of a job doesn't correlate to how others view it.

You bring value to your job. You find its meaning—or no one does.

If it falls to your lot to be a street sweeper, sweep streets like Michelangelo carved marble. Sweep streets as Shakespeare wrote pictures. Sweep streets so well that all the hosts of heaven will have to say, "Here lives the streetsweeper who did his job well."
—Martin Luther King, Jr.

Self-Satisfied

Complacency is the worst disease and the biggest sin—the ultimate blindness.

If you're unwilling to see how you fail, you can't improve.

If you're unwilling to see your shortcomings, you can't grow.

If you're satisfied with yourself, you become self-satisfied.

I am always doing that which I cannot do,
in order that I may learn how to do it.
—Pablo Picasso

Money

When you count your riches in money, do this: Count, too, your riches in health, education, talent, respect, beauty, delight, laughter and love.

That I exist is a perpetual surprise, which is life.—Rabindranath Tagore

The Lesson of Laundry

The lesson of doing the laundry is that the machines can't be hurried.

You're stuck there waiting for the cycles to be done.

You can't put on the gas and pick up a little speed. You can't cut corners. You can't cheat.

You wait.

And if you're looking for it, you find in the enforced stillness the space to breathe. And think. And be.

Our life is frittered away by detail....Simplify, simplify.—Henry David Thoreau

St. Scrooge

Dickens called Scrooge "an old sinner." And so he was. He was greedy and cold-hearted and miserly and mean.

But he repented. He saw the error of his ways.

He admitted his failure and changed his life.

None of us is without sin.

Each of us has the chance to change.

Good people are good because they've come to wisdom through failure. We get very little wisdom from success, you know.
—William Saroyan

Romance

Love is a dance. Love talks without words. Love reveals and risks. Love is a simple, gentle touch.

Love is the river of life in the world.
—*Henry Ward Beecher*

The Feast of Life

Each beginning has an end.

Each morning has an evening.

Each birth has a death.

Don't hide from life. Don't run from experience. Don't fear failure or pain or embarrassment.

Embrace life. It's a messy proposition. Yet, for all its ugliness, there is great beauty. For all its pain, there is great joy.

Revel in the richness of life. Feast at life's table.

A cheerful heart has a continual feast.
—Proverbs 15:15